LIVE THE LIFE YOU HAVE IMAGINED COMPANION JOURNAL!

Your Personal Guide to Begin Living Your Best Life

Janie Jurkovich

Live the Life You Have Imagined Companion Journal!
Your Personal Guide to Begin Living Your Best Life

By Janie Jurkovich

Copyright © 2019

Golden Spiral Press ™ is a trademark of Janie Jurkovich

Editing & Project Management by Beth Bridges, eBridge Marketing

Cover, Logo & Chart Design by Ellie Dote, Ellie Girl Creations

Interior Design by Bryan Keith Pfeifer

Author Photo by Suzanne Moles, Wattleweb Global Solutions

First Edition: January 2019
Published by Golden Spiral Press
Fresno, California
www.JanieJ.net

This journal belongs to

_____

I began living my best life on

_____

I last reviewed my progress on

_____

_____

_____

_____

_____

_____

DEDICATION

For you: someone who is ready to take action and live the life they have always imagined!

Contents

TIME AND PATIENCE

Want a better life?
Don't we all.
What are you waiting for -
A personal call?

What are you willing to give?
How much can you take?
To meet that goal
There's a price to pay.

It's paid with effort.
It's paid with sweat.
Keep on trying
Till the goal is met.

Time and patience
Will take care of the rest.

~ Janie J

INTRODUCTION

I started writing the blog posts that would eventually become "Live the Life You Have Imagined: Simple Ways to Begin Living Your Best Life" while driving. Not literally. But it all started during a drive.

My mind was in turmoil one day while I was on my way to one of my commercial properties. Less than one year earlier, my husband had unexpectedly left me.

After 35 years of marriage, devoting myself to family and home, with a career on the side, I was suddenly lost. Where was the life I imagined I would have? What happened to all my dreams? When did I lose sight of myself?

All these thoughts and more were tumbling around in my head. Suddenly, I started thinking about the things I needed to do to turn my life around. It was nothing short of a divine download into my mind, so I pulled over to the side of the road and wrote furiously for 40 minutes.

Those scribbled thoughts became short weekly posts on LinkedIn and Facebook.

Friends started responding to them and I realized I wasn't the only one who was wondering how to live a better life.

After only a few posts, my now ex-husband felt it necessary to comment on a post to ridicule me. "What are you doing? Why are you even bothering with this?" he said. I was astonished. He couldn't understand how I might want to improve myself and to work on living a better life.

It helped me realize two things: he had done me a favor by leaving and I needed to get this message into the hands of women who were, like me, searching for answers.

That's how my book "Live the Life You Have Imagined: Simple Ways to Begin Living Your Best Life" came into being. If you don't have it, you'll want to get a copy now before you start to using this companion journal. You can get it at **https://amzn.to/2MXtLz2** in print on Amazon.com, as a Kindle ebook to begin reading it right now, or as an audio book if you like to listen.

How to Use This Journal

If you haven't already read "Live the Life You Have Imagined: Simple Ways to Begin Living Your Best Life," do that before anything else. Read all the way through at least once. It's a very quick and straightforward book. You could probably finish it in a few days.

Then spend some time just reflecting, imagining and even daydreaming before you dive into this companion journal.

Give yourself a few days to dream… and fantasize… and imagine living YOUR best life.

Don't get carried away and then set this book down to never pick it up again! That's how so many of us spend years or even decades living someone else's dream or just sleepwalking through our own lives.

We Think and Daydream But We Never DO

Put it on your calendar to pick up this companion journal and start using it. You might make a weekly appointment with yourself. Create a recurring calendar event and block out that time so nothing interferes with living your best life.

Even better, find a few like-minded friends and start a discussion group. Plan to meet weekly and keep each other accountable for reading, thinking and doing.

Keep the book nearby for constant reference. Personally, even though I wrote it, I STILL go back and review certain chapters. This companion journal will help you know where you're reaching your goals and where you need to continue to focus.

Each chapter in this companion guide corresponds to the chapter in the book. There is a quick summary followed by the discussion questions in each chapter. You might already have written down your answers in your copy of "Live the Life You Have Imagined" (or you might have downloaded the free, printable copy of the questions here: www.JanieJ.net/bonus).

You can rewrite your answers (or maybe they've already changed) in this companion journal. Or, if you didn't have time to answer the questions, that's your first step.

You can do all the questions in all 31 chapters, but I think that will be overwhelming. I recommend you start with chapters 2, 3 and 4.

I consider that triad to be the foundation of everything else in my book. These are "keystone habits" which are certain actions that - once in place - will lead to success in many other areas of your life.

It works in reverse, too. You almost can't function if you don't have these three things in place or if you're struggling with them. If these are a challenge for you, allow yourself plenty of time before trying to tackle everything else. Don't be frustrated... it's normal and these might be big changes for you. But once you get these dialed in, the rest of the activities will be much easier and you'll see faster progress after you've got the triad in place.

Start with the Discussion Questions

Answer the questions for each chapter on your own or with your discussion group. Be sure to write your thoughts down, don't just think about it in your head. Writing it down will help you clarify what you need to do and will help you **remember** what you want to do. Plus, you'll be able to see changes in your thinking when you review at 3, 6, 9 and 12 months. For example, problems or obstacles that you write down now may seem so simple or will entirely disappear.

If you don't have enough room to write, you can download all of the discussion questions for free at **www.JanieJ.net/bonus**

Evaluate Where You Are Now

After the questions, each chapter gives you an assessment scale for where you are now, then at 3, 6, 9 and 12 months. Make a calendar reminder to take a few minutes to evaluate your progress each quarter.

It's okay if you don't make progress on every single thing. Don't expect to be in the final column ("Integrated into my Daily Life") in everything in just one year. If you are, congratulations, you're Superwoman!

For the rest of us, it's going to be a journey. This was a long process for me. I'm still working on many of these things. You might make slow progress. You will probably have setbacks and will have to reprioritize. I expect this to be a lifetime project for myself and you should too.

So remember, don't get discouraged if you don't make progress on every single thing every quarter!

It's okay to not make progress. Don't beat yourself up or consider this a failure.

Most people are going to be doing very well to read most of the book and apply some of these strategies. As I said earlier, start by focusing on chapter 2, 3 and 4. If you can dial these in, you will be making great progress.

Track Your Habits

Use "My Habits" to keep track of a habit you are trying to develop. Pull out the page (or make a copy) and post it where you usually do (or want to do) the habit. Then use a big, bright colored marker to check off each day that you complete that habit.

Research shows that it takes anywhere from 18 to 254 days to form a new habit. My tracking sheet has you aiming for 21 days because it's very doable and you can form a new habit in that time if you keep it simple.

Don't overwhelm yourself. Focus on just one or two habits at a time.

Focus + Habit => Results

You can also improve your chances of success by choosing very small habits at first. So instead of "completely remove all refined carbohydrates" try "don't add sugar to my coffee."

It's easier to add a habit of doing something positive instead of trying to remove a bad habit. Try to find good habits that replace a bad one. "Meditate for five minutes before bed" is a positive habit that might also replace "don't watch TV in bed."

Download a completely blank, printable "My Habits" form from my website at **www.JanieJ.net/bonus2**

MY HABITS

Focus + Habits = Results
You can use a chekmark, star, or X on each day you complete the habit.
Make it a big, bold mark in a bright color.

Eat an apple or banana or carrots as a snack 1x a day

| ☒ 1 | ☒ 2 | ☒ 3 | ☐ 4 | ☐ 5 | ☐ 6 | ☐ 7 | ☐ 8 | ☐ 9 | ☐ 10 | ☐ 11 |
| ☐ 12 | ☐ 13 | ☐ 14 | ☐ 15 | ☐ 16 | ☐ 17 | ☐ 18 | ☐ 19 | ☐ 20 | ☐ 21 | |

| ☐ 1 | ☐ 2 | ☐ 3 | ☐ 4 | ☐ 5 | ☐ 6 | ☐ 7 | ☐ 8 | ☐ 9 | ☐ 10 | ☐ 11 |
| ☐ 12 | ☐ 13 | ☐ 14 | ☐ 15 | ☐ 16 | ☐ 17 | ☐ 18 | ☐ 19 | ☐ 20 | ☐ 21 | |

| ☐ 1 | ☐ 2 | ☐ 3 | ☐ 4 | ☐ 5 | ☐ 6 | ☐ 7 | ☐ 8 | ☐ 9 | ☐ 10 | ☐ 11 |
| ☐ 12 | ☐ 13 | ☐ 14 | ☐ 15 | ☐ 16 | ☐ 17 | ☐ 18 | ☐ 19 | ☐ 20 | ☐ 21 | |

| ☐ 1 | ☐ 2 | ☐ 3 | ☐ 4 | ☐ 5 | ☐ 6 | ☐ 7 | ☐ 8 | ☐ 9 | ☐ 10 | ☐ 11 |
| ☐ 12 | ☐ 13 | ☐ 14 | ☐ 15 | ☐ 16 | ☐ 17 | ☐ 18 | ☐ 19 | ☐ 20 | ☐ 21 | |

| ☐ 1 | ☐ 2 | ☐ 3 | ☐ 4 | ☐ 5 | ☐ 6 | ☐ 7 | ☐ 8 | ☐ 9 | ☐ 10 | ☐ 11 |
| ☐ 12 | ☐ 13 | ☐ 14 | ☐ 15 | ☐ 16 | ☐ 17 | ☐ 18 | ☐ 19 | ☐ 20 | ☐ 21 | |

| ☐ 1 | ☐ 2 | ☐ 3 | ☐ 4 | ☐ 5 | ☐ 6 | ☐ 7 | ☐ 8 | ☐ 9 | ☐ 10 | ☐ 11 |
| ☐ 12 | ☐ 13 | ☐ 14 | ☐ 15 | ☐ 16 | ☐ 17 | ☐ 18 | ☐ 19 | ☐ 20 | ☐ 21 | |

| ☐ 1 | ☐ 2 | ☐ 3 | ☐ 4 | ☐ 5 | ☐ 6 | ☐ 7 | ☐ 8 | ☐ 9 | ☐ 10 | ☐ 11 |
| ☐ 12 | ☐ 13 | ☐ 14 | ☐ 15 | ☐ 16 | ☐ 17 | ☐ 18 | ☐ 19 | ☐ 20 | ☐ 21 | |

| ☐ 1 | ☐ 2 | ☐ 3 | ☐ 4 | ☐ 5 | ☐ 6 | ☐ 7 | ☐ 8 | ☐ 9 | ☐ 10 | ☐ 11 |
| ☐ 12 | ☐ 13 | ☐ 14 | ☐ 15 | ☐ 16 | ☐ 17 | ☐ 18 | ☐ 19 | ☐ 20 | ☐ 21 | |

| ☐ 1 | ☐ 2 | ☐ 3 | ☐ 4 | ☐ 5 | ☐ 6 | ☐ 7 | ☐ 8 | ☐ 9 | ☐ 10 | ☐ 11 |
| ☐ 12 | ☐ 13 | ☐ 14 | ☐ 15 | ☐ 16 | ☐ 17 | ☐ 18 | ☐ 19 | ☐ 20 | ☐ 21 | |

| ☐ 1 | ☐ 2 | ☐ 3 | ☐ 4 | ☐ 5 | ☐ 6 | ☐ 7 | ☐ 8 | ☐ 9 | ☐ 10 | ☐ 11 |
| ☐ 12 | ☐ 13 | ☐ 14 | ☐ 15 | ☐ 16 | ☐ 17 | ☐ 18 | ☐ 19 | ☐ 20 | ☐ 21 | |

Live the Life
YOU
HAVE IMAGINED!

Celebrate Your Successes

This is something that we often forget to do, but it's very important. When you've accomplished something, write it down. For example, "got 7 hours of sleep every night for a week." Or "turned off the TV at 8 p.m. 5 days in a row."

These might seem like very small wins, but don't wait for the huge accomplishment to celebrate and encourage yourself.

This is not about mastery, it's about progress.

Download a completely blank, printable form from my website at
www.JanieJ.net/bonus2

——— MY SUCCESSES ———

Celebrate successes, wins and achievements no matter how small.

Description	Date
Got 7 hours of sleep for 7 days	Dec. 7-13, 2018
Responded calmly to "drama" coworker	Jan. 5, 2019

Live the Life
YOU
HAVE IMAGINED!

How to Use This Companion Journal in a Book Club

Do you want to 10X your results and get closer to the life you imagined even faster? Then find or create an accountability group or start a book club of your own.

Start by talking to your friends and business connections who might be in a similar place as you: divorced, widowed, experiencing other big changes in her life or just feeling stuck and ready for change.

It might be hard for them (and you) to admit that you're not happy where you are, but if you're willing to take the risk and open up, you'll probably find several enthusiastic friends.

Be open, but also be selective in who you invite. You need people who are positive, encouraging and ready to make changes in their life.

Studies show that some people have friends who actively sabotage their progress in losing weight for example because those friends feel insecure about their own lives.

Find a time to meet once a week or every other week at the least. Once a month is not often enough. You'll lose track of what you're working on and it will be hard to sustain momentum.

Don't feel obligated to share where you are if you're not comfortable. Instead, focus on encouraging each other and helping to find solutions or ideas for overcoming obstacles. Be sure to celebrate your wins. Set a meeting each quarter aside just for completing your personal progress evaluations.

Remember, this will be tough. People will get discouraged. Life will happen. You'll all miss a meeting or two or ten. Keep persevering, though, and at the end of a year you will all make measurable changes.

Celebrate! Have a wonderful lunch or dinner together to acknowledge your hard work and your success.

Isn't this much more like the life you always imagined living?

Now… keep going!

Narrow Your Focus to Be Successful

To help you keep your focus narrowed down, use this chart to decide what is a priority for you right now. Do this *after* you've read the book "Live the Life You Imagined" but *before* you start evaluating each chapter. Make a copy of this page if you want to reevaluate this once or twice a year.

Choose Your Priorities

Pick just a FEW things to work on at a time. Put a checkmark or X in the boxes to help you stay focused on your top priorities.

Once you know where your priorities are, get started with those chapters by answering the discussion questions and evaluating where you are right now.

I know you can do this! Even if you don't complete everything or even make progress on everything, if you just do *some* work, in 3 months you are going to be in a better place than you are now.

You'll be that much closer to living the life you imagined.

Let's get you started!

NARROW YOUR FOCUS
TO BE SUCCESSFUL

CHAPTER	TOP PRIORITY	IMPORTANT BUT LATER	NOT IMPORTANT	ALREADY DOING
1 Live the Life				
2 First Step				
3 Sleep	✓			
4 Eat Healthy	✓			
5 Exercise	✓			
6 Meditate				
7 Read				
8 Say "No"				
9 Work/Life Harmony				
10 Downtime				
11 Mix It Up				
12 Clutter				
13 "In the Moment"				
14 Delegate				
15 Comfort Zone				
16 Perseverance				

CHAPTER	TOP PRIORITY	IMPORTANT BUT LATER	NOT IMPORTANT	ALREADY DOING
17 Music!				
18 Change				
19 Ignore Naysayers				
20 The High Road				
21 Attitude				
22 Gratitude				
23 Lessons				
24 Challenges				
25 Laugh				
26 Wealth				
27 Delete TV				
28 Follow Bliss				
29 Self-Development				
30 The Journey				
31 Components				

CHAPTER ONE

MY LIFE AS I IMAGINED

"If one advances confidently in the direction of her dreams, and endeavors to live the life which she has imagined, she will meet with success unexpected in common hours." - Henry David Thoreau

1. Are you living the life you have imagined?
2. If you could magically make it happen right now, what would it look like? Describe it in as much detail as you can.

The Life I Imagine:

MY LIFE AS I IMAGINED

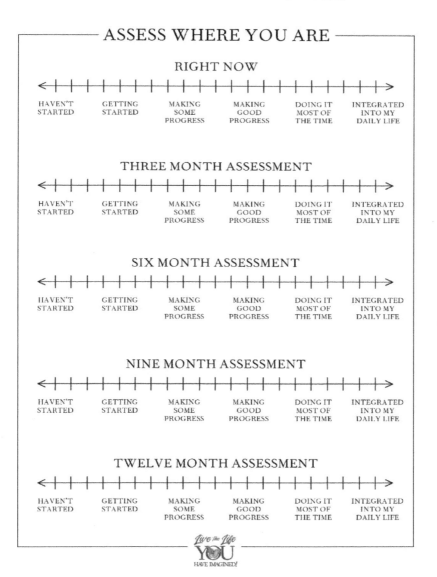

ASSESS WHERE YOU ARE

RIGHT NOW

| HAVEN'T STARTED | GETTING STARTED | MAKING SOME PROGRESS | MAKING GOOD PROGRESS | DOING IT MOST OF THE TIME | INTEGRATED INTO MY DAILY LIFE |

THREE MONTH ASSESSMENT

| HAVEN'T STARTED | GETTING STARTED | MAKING SOME PROGRESS | MAKING GOOD PROGRESS | DOING IT MOST OF THE TIME | INTEGRATED INTO MY DAILY LIFE |

SIX MONTH ASSESSMENT

| HAVEN'T STARTED | GETTING STARTED | MAKING SOME PROGRESS | MAKING GOOD PROGRESS | DOING IT MOST OF THE TIME | INTEGRATED INTO MY DAILY LIFE |

NINE MONTH ASSESSMENT

| HAVEN'T STARTED | GETTING STARTED | MAKING SOME PROGRESS | MAKING GOOD PROGRESS | DOING IT MOST OF THE TIME | INTEGRATED INTO MY DAILY LIFE |

TWELVE MONTH ASSESSMENT

| HAVEN'T STARTED | GETTING STARTED | MAKING SOME PROGRESS | MAKING GOOD PROGRESS | DOING IT MOST OF THE TIME | INTEGRATED INTO MY DAILY LIFE |

Live the Life
YOU
HAVE IMAGINED!

23

CHAPTER TWO

THE FIRST STEP

"The first step toward getting somewhere is to decide that you are not going to stay where you are."
- J. Pierpont Morgan

1. How did your two lists of your daily life NOW versus what you would LIKE compare? Were they fairly close or way off?
2. What did this exercise teach you about how you are living now? Is it all off-the cuff emergencies or is it purposeful?
3. What adjustments can you make to your current life easily and start incorporating into your daily routine?
4. What long-term goal or goals did you set? Are they stretch-goals, or easier, more attainable ones?
5. Give an example of the steps to achieve one of your goals.

Remember, these questions are based on the information and stories in my book "Live the Life You Have Imagined: Simple Ways to Begin Living Your Best Life" available on Amazon at amzn.to/2MXtLz2

My Goals:

THE FIRST STEP

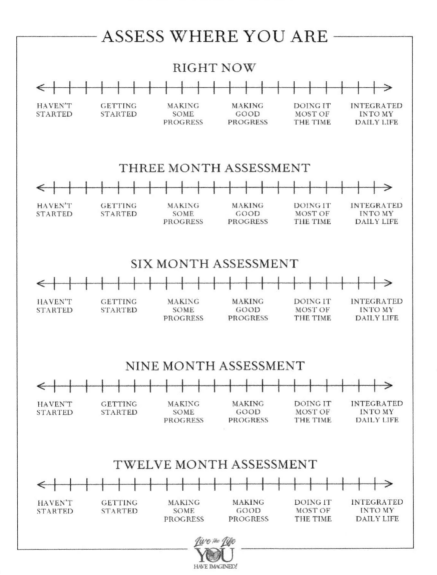

ASSESS WHERE YOU ARE

RIGHT NOW

HAVEN'T STARTED   GETTING STARTED   MAKING SOME PROGRESS   MAKING GOOD PROGRESS   DOING IT MOST OF THE TIME   INTEGRATED INTO MY DAILY LIFE

THREE MONTH ASSESSMENT

HAVEN'T STARTED   GETTING STARTED   MAKING SOME PROGRESS   MAKING GOOD PROGRESS   DOING IT MOST OF THE TIME   INTEGRATED INTO MY DAILY LIFE

SIX MONTH ASSESSMENT

HAVEN'T STARTED   GETTING STARTED   MAKING SOME PROGRESS   MAKING GOOD PROGRESS   DOING IT MOST OF THE TIME   INTEGRATED INTO MY DAILY LIFE

NINE MONTH ASSESSMENT

HAVEN'T STARTED   GETTING STARTED   MAKING SOME PROGRESS   MAKING GOOD PROGRESS   DOING IT MOST OF THE TIME   INTEGRATED INTO MY DAILY LIFE

TWELVE MONTH ASSESSMENT

HAVEN'T STARTED   GETTING STARTED   MAKING SOME PROGRESS   MAKING GOOD PROGRESS   DOING IT MOST OF THE TIME   INTEGRATED INTO MY DAILY LIFE

Live the Life
YOU
HAVE IMAGINED!

CHAPTER THREE

SLEEP

"The way to a more productive, more inspired, more joyful life is getting enough sleep."
- Arianna Huffington

1. How did you determine the right amount of sleep for you?
2. What happens if you DON'T get enough sleep? What happens when you DO get enough sleep?
3. Do you notice any changes in your levels of competency and/or attitude when you lack sufficient sleep?
4. What can you do to ensure you get enough sleep? Any tips to share?

My Plan For Proper Sleep:

SLEEP

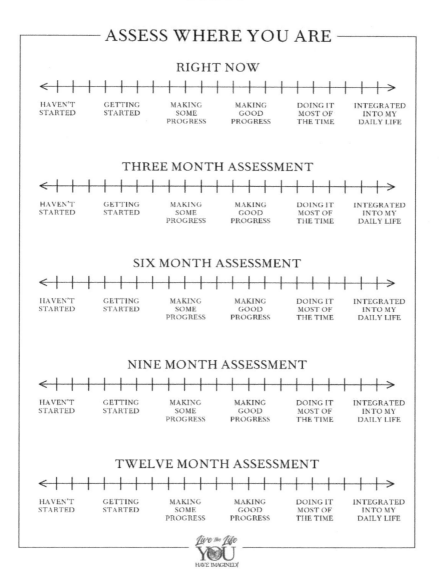

ASSESS WHERE YOU ARE

RIGHT NOW

HAVEN'T STARTED — GETTING STARTED — MAKING SOME PROGRESS — MAKING GOOD PROGRESS — DOING IT MOST OF THE TIME — INTEGRATED INTO MY DAILY LIFE

THREE MONTH ASSESSMENT

HAVEN'T STARTED — GETTING STARTED — MAKING SOME PROGRESS — MAKING GOOD PROGRESS — DOING IT MOST OF THE TIME — INTEGRATED INTO MY DAILY LIFE

SIX MONTH ASSESSMENT

HAVEN'T STARTED — GETTING STARTED — MAKING SOME PROGRESS — MAKING GOOD PROGRESS — DOING IT MOST OF THE TIME — INTEGRATED INTO MY DAILY LIFE

NINE MONTH ASSESSMENT

HAVEN'T STARTED — GETTING STARTED — MAKING SOME PROGRESS — MAKING GOOD PROGRESS — DOING IT MOST OF THE TIME — INTEGRATED INTO MY DAILY LIFE

TWELVE MONTH ASSESSMENT

HAVEN'T STARTED — GETTING STARTED — MAKING SOME PROGRESS — MAKING GOOD PROGRESS — DOING IT MOST OF THE TIME — INTEGRATED INTO MY DAILY LIFE

Live the Life
YOU
HAVE IMAGINED!

CHAPTER FOUR

EAT HEALTHY

"Healthy eating is a way of life, so it's important to establish routines that are simple, realistically, and ultimately livable." - Arthur Agatston

1. What one action could you take to improve your eating habits?
2. Give some examples of changes you have made to improve your eating habits.
3. Share some of your meal preparation tips with the group.
4. What steps have you taken to enlist the help of others with meal preparation?
5. Figure out how much you spend on eating out each month versus buying groceries. Think about what you could spend that money on instead.
6. What healthy options have you found at the grocery store or restaurants?

My Eating Plan:

EAT HEALTHY

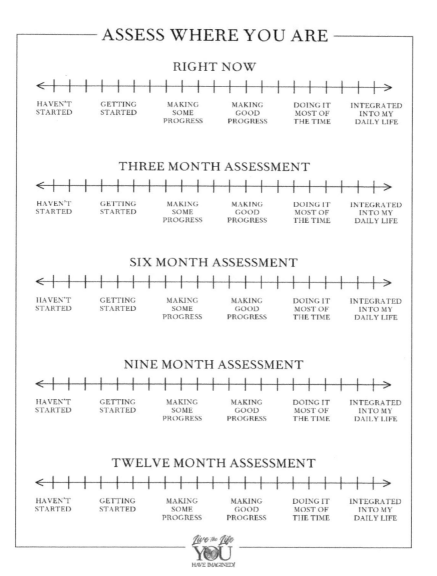

ASSESS WHERE YOU ARE

RIGHT NOW

HAVEN'T STARTED   GETTING STARTED   MAKING SOME PROGRESS   MAKING GOOD PROGRESS   DOING IT MOST OF THE TIME   INTEGRATED INTO MY DAILY LIFE

THREE MONTH ASSESSMENT

HAVEN'T STARTED   GETTING STARTED   MAKING SOME PROGRESS   MAKING GOOD PROGRESS   DOING IT MOST OF THE TIME   INTEGRATED INTO MY DAILY LIFE

SIX MONTH ASSESSMENT

HAVEN'T STARTED   GETTING STARTED   MAKING SOME PROGRESS   MAKING GOOD PROGRESS   DOING IT MOST OF THE TIME   INTEGRATED INTO MY DAILY LIFE

NINE MONTH ASSESSMENT

HAVEN'T STARTED   GETTING STARTED   MAKING SOME PROGRESS   MAKING GOOD PROGRESS   DOING IT MOST OF THE TIME   INTEGRATED INTO MY DAILY LIFE

TWELVE MONTH ASSESSMENT

HAVEN'T STARTED   GETTING STARTED   MAKING SOME PROGRESS   MAKING GOOD PROGRESS   DOING IT MOST OF THE TIME   INTEGRATED INTO MY DAILY LIFE

Live the Life YOU HAVE IMAGINED!

JANIE JURKOVICH

CHAPTER FIVE

EXERCISE

"Physical fitness is not only one of the most important keys to a healthy body, it is the basis of dynamic and creative intellectual activity." - John F. Kennedy

1. What is your motivation for exercising?
2. What type of activities do you prefer? Do you like group or individual activities?
3. How can you make exercise a regular part of your life?
4. When do you plan to exercise – morning, afternoon, evening or other?

My Exercise Plan:

EXERCISE

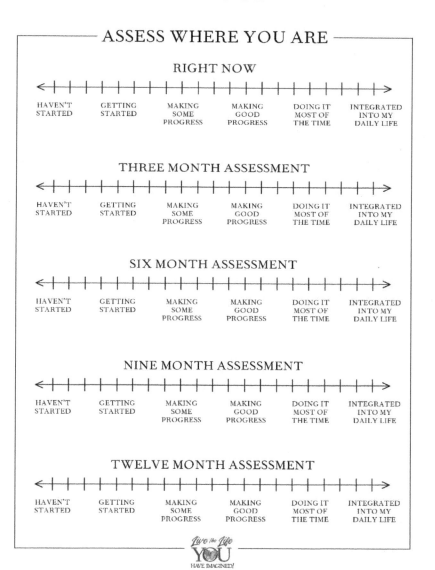

ASSESS WHERE YOU ARE

RIGHT NOW

| HAVEN'T STARTED | GETTING STARTED | MAKING SOME PROGRESS | MAKING GOOD PROGRESS | DOING IT MOST OF THE TIME | INTEGRATED INTO MY DAILY LIFE |

THREE MONTH ASSESSMENT

| HAVEN'T STARTED | GETTING STARTED | MAKING SOME PROGRESS | MAKING GOOD PROGRESS | DOING IT MOST OF THE TIME | INTEGRATED INTO MY DAILY LIFE |

SIX MONTH ASSESSMENT

| HAVEN'T STARTED | GETTING STARTED | MAKING SOME PROGRESS | MAKING GOOD PROGRESS | DOING IT MOST OF THE TIME | INTEGRATED INTO MY DAILY LIFE |

NINE MONTH ASSESSMENT

| HAVEN'T STARTED | GETTING STARTED | MAKING SOME PROGRESS | MAKING GOOD PROGRESS | DOING IT MOST OF THE TIME | INTEGRATED INTO MY DAILY LIFE |

TWELVE MONTH ASSESSMENT

| HAVEN'T STARTED | GETTING STARTED | MAKING SOME PROGRESS | MAKING GOOD PROGRESS | DOING IT MOST OF THE TIME | INTEGRATED INTO MY DAILY LIFE |

Live the life YOU HAVE IMAGINED!

CHAPTER SIX

MEDITATE

"The quieter you become, the more you hear."
- Baba Ram Dass

1. Do you practice meditation or quiet time regularly? If so, what is your style of meditating? (There is no right answer.) Are you aware there are many types of mediation from different cultures and religions?

2. Where do you or could you easily and comfortably practice meditation?

3. When is a good time for you to meditate?

4. What changes could you make to fit in a little time for yourself to meditate?

5. What benefits have you gained from meditating?

My Meditation Plan:

MEDITATE

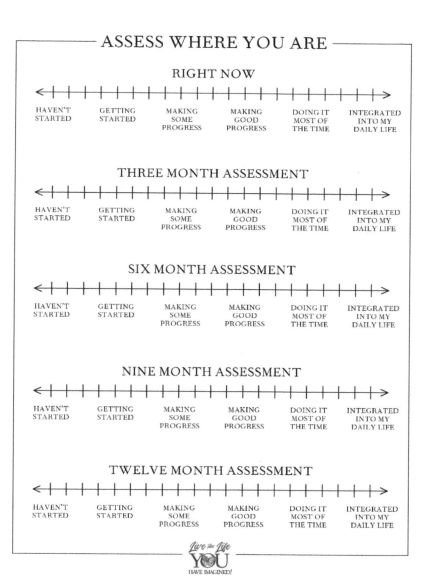

ASSESS WHERE YOU ARE

RIGHT NOW

| HAVEN'T STARTED | GETTING STARTED | MAKING SOME PROGRESS | MAKING GOOD PROGRESS | DOING IT MOST OF THE TIME | INTEGRATED INTO MY DAILY LIFE |

THREE MONTH ASSESSMENT

| HAVEN'T STARTED | GETTING STARTED | MAKING SOME PROGRESS | MAKING GOOD PROGRESS | DOING IT MOST OF THE TIME | INTEGRATED INTO MY DAILY LIFE |

SIX MONTH ASSESSMENT

| HAVEN'T STARTED | GETTING STARTED | MAKING SOME PROGRESS | MAKING GOOD PROGRESS | DOING IT MOST OF THE TIME | INTEGRATED INTO MY DAILY LIFE |

NINE MONTH ASSESSMENT

| HAVEN'T STARTED | GETTING STARTED | MAKING SOME PROGRESS | MAKING GOOD PROGRESS | DOING IT MOST OF THE TIME | INTEGRATED INTO MY DAILY LIFE |

TWELVE MONTH ASSESSMENT

| HAVEN'T STARTED | GETTING STARTED | MAKING SOME PROGRESS | MAKING GOOD PROGRESS | DOING IT MOST OF THE TIME | INTEGRATED INTO MY DAILY LIFE |

Live the Life YOU HAVE IMAGINED!

CHAPTER SEVEN

READ DAILY

"The man who does not read good books is no better than the man who can't." - Mark Twain

1. How and when were you able to set aside reading time?
2. Give an example of some of the books or articles you have read.
3. What topic have you read about that sparked an interest for future exploration?
4. Have any articles or books changed your mind or offered insights?

My Reading Plan:

READ DAILY

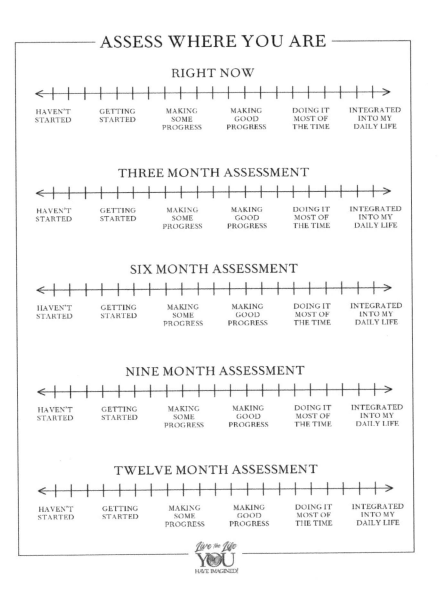

ASSESS WHERE YOU ARE

RIGHT NOW

HAVEN'T STARTED   GETTING STARTED   MAKING SOME PROGRESS   MAKING GOOD PROGRESS   DOING IT MOST OF THE TIME   INTEGRATED INTO MY DAILY LIFE

THREE MONTH ASSESSMENT

HAVEN'T STARTED   GETTING STARTED   MAKING SOME PROGRESS   MAKING GOOD PROGRESS   DOING IT MOST OF THE TIME   INTEGRATED INTO MY DAILY LIFE

SIX MONTH ASSESSMENT

HAVEN'T STARTED   GETTING STARTED   MAKING SOME PROGRESS   MAKING GOOD PROGRESS   DOING IT MOST OF THE TIME   INTEGRATED INTO MY DAILY LIFE

NINE MONTH ASSESSMENT

HAVEN'T STARTED   GETTING STARTED   MAKING SOME PROGRESS   MAKING GOOD PROGRESS   DOING IT MOST OF THE TIME   INTEGRATED INTO MY DAILY LIFE

TWELVE MONTH ASSESSMENT

HAVEN'T STARTED   GETTING STARTED   MAKING SOME PROGRESS   MAKING GOOD PROGRESS   DOING IT MOST OF THE TIME   INTEGRATED INTO MY DAILY LIFE

Live the Life
YOU
HAVE IMAGINED!

JANIE JURKOVICH

CHAPTER EIGHT

SAY "NO" TO THE SHOULDS

"It's only by saying 'no' that you can concentrate on the things that are really important." - Steve Jobs

1. What activities could you say "No" to?

2. How much time do you spend each week doing "No" items?

3. What could you have done with that time if you had the courage to say "No"?

4. After answering these questions, do you think you could move more items to the "No" side?

My Plan for Saying "No:" *(Write some suggested scripts)*

SAY "NO" TO THE SHOULDS

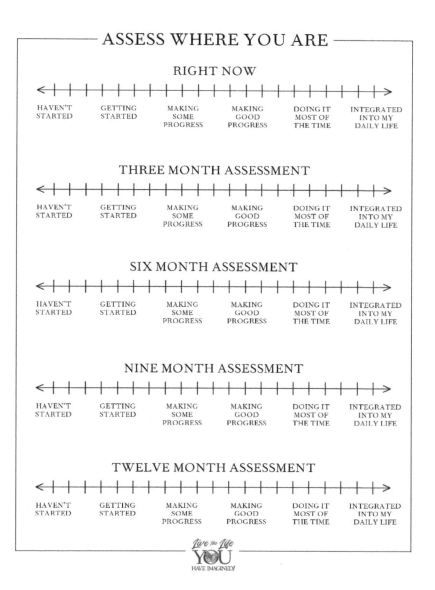

ASSESS WHERE YOU ARE

RIGHT NOW

HAVEN'T STARTED   GETTING STARTED   MAKING SOME PROGRESS   MAKING GOOD PROGRESS   DOING IT MOST OF THE TIME   INTEGRATED INTO MY DAILY LIFE

THREE MONTH ASSESSMENT

HAVEN'T STARTED   GETTING STARTED   MAKING SOME PROGRESS   MAKING GOOD PROGRESS   DOING IT MOST OF THE TIME   INTEGRATED INTO MY DAILY LIFE

SIX MONTH ASSESSMENT

HAVEN'T STARTED   GETTING STARTED   MAKING SOME PROGRESS   MAKING GOOD PROGRESS   DOING IT MOST OF THE TIME   INTEGRATED INTO MY DAILY LIFE

NINE MONTH ASSESSMENT

HAVEN'T STARTED   GETTING STARTED   MAKING SOME PROGRESS   MAKING GOOD PROGRESS   DOING IT MOST OF THE TIME   INTEGRATED INTO MY DAILY LIFE

TWELVE MONTH ASSESSMENT

HAVEN'T STARTED   GETTING STARTED   MAKING SOME PROGRESS   MAKING GOOD PROGRESS   DOING IT MOST OF THE TIME   INTEGRATED INTO MY DAILY LIFE

Live the Life
YOU
HAVE IMAGINED!

CHAPTER NINE

STRIVE FOR WORK/LIFE HARMONY, NOT BALANCE

"Realize that work-life balance is elusive and find harmony in everything you do." - Adriana Girdler

1. What work/life challenges have you encountered?
2. How have you handled them?
3. Do you ever feel guilty or incompetent? (Recognize when this happens and resolve not to let it guide you to do things you do not really have to do.)
4. How would a different perspective help you see such challenges in a new light?

My Plan to Deal with Work/Life Harmony: *(List priorities or scenarios that might help you focus on this skill)*

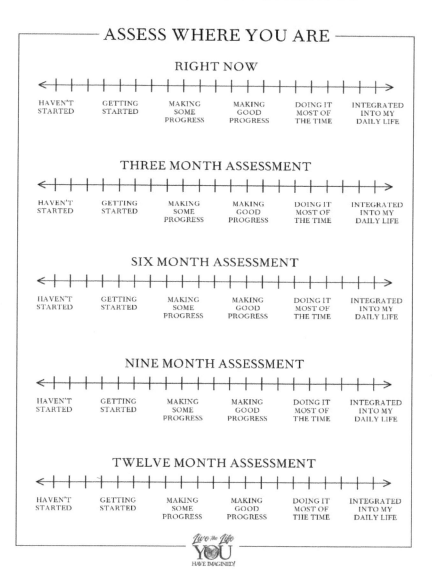

LIVE THE LIFE YOU HAVE IMAGINED!

STRIVE FOR WORK/LIFE HARMONY, NOT BALANCE

ASSESS WHERE YOU ARE

RIGHT NOW

| HAVEN'T STARTED | GETTING STARTED | MAKING SOME PROGRESS | MAKING GOOD PROGRESS | DOING IT MOST OF THE TIME | INTEGRATED INTO MY DAILY LIFE |

THREE MONTH ASSESSMENT

| HAVEN'T STARTED | GETTING STARTED | MAKING SOME PROGRESS | MAKING GOOD PROGRESS | DOING IT MOST OF THE TIME | INTEGRATED INTO MY DAILY LIFE |

SIX MONTH ASSESSMENT

| HAVEN'T STARTED | GETTING STARTED | MAKING SOME PROGRESS | MAKING GOOD PROGRESS | DOING IT MOST OF THE TIME | INTEGRATED INTO MY DAILY LIFE |

NINE MONTH ASSESSMENT

| HAVEN'T STARTED | GETTING STARTED | MAKING SOME PROGRESS | MAKING GOOD PROGRESS | DOING IT MOST OF THE TIME | INTEGRATED INTO MY DAILY LIFE |

TWELVE MONTH ASSESSMENT

| HAVEN'T STARTED | GETTING STARTED | MAKING SOME PROGRESS | MAKING GOOD PROGRESS | DOING IT MOST OF THE TIME | INTEGRATED INTO MY DAILY LIFE |

Live the Life
YOU
HAVE IMAGINED!

JANIE JURKOVICH

CHAPTER TEN

SCHEDULE DOWNTIME

"Humans are just like smartphones or iPods: We have
to be recharged, or we run out of juice."
- Saurabh Bhatia

1. If money and time were no object, daydream about the vacations you would take. Write a list. Pick one or two for this year and put it on your calendar. Figure out when, where, the budget, and possible ways to fund it.

2. Spend one to two minutes writing a list of fun activities that you enjoy or would like to try. Write as fast as you can without thinking about the practicality of each item. Include things from watching the sunrise/sunset, walking the dog, a late-night swim, coffee with a girlfriend, skydiving, hitting golf balls, to taking horseback riding lesson. Later you can edit and prioritize the list. Pick a few to do this week and add them to your schedule. Make it happen!

3. Think about how you felt planning these vacations and mini-vacations? Was your mood lifted? Are you happier and more positive? (You are likely already feeling the benefits of having some downtime.)

4. What vacation and fun activity are you now COMMITTED to doing?

My Downtime Plan:

SCHEDULE DOWNTIME

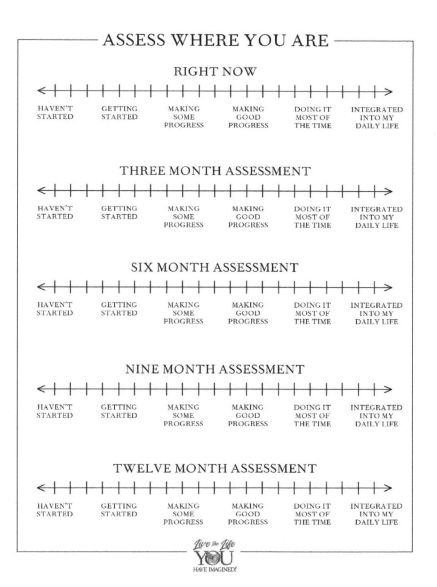

ASSESS WHERE YOU ARE

RIGHT NOW

HAVEN'T STARTED   GETTING STARTED   MAKING SOME PROGRESS   MAKING GOOD PROGRESS   DOING IT MOST OF THE TIME   INTEGRATED INTO MY DAILY LIFE

THREE MONTH ASSESSMENT

HAVEN'T STARTED   GETTING STARTED   MAKING SOME PROGRESS   MAKING GOOD PROGRESS   DOING IT MOST OF THE TIME   INTEGRATED INTO MY DAILY LIFE

SIX MONTH ASSESSMENT

HAVEN'T STARTED   GETTING STARTED   MAKING SOME PROGRESS   MAKING GOOD PROGRESS   DOING IT MOST OF THE TIME   INTEGRATED INTO MY DAILY LIFE

NINE MONTH ASSESSMENT

HAVEN'T STARTED   GETTING STARTED   MAKING SOME PROGRESS   MAKING GOOD PROGRESS   DOING IT MOST OF THE TIME   INTEGRATED INTO MY DAILY LIFE

TWELVE MONTH ASSESSMENT

HAVEN'T STARTED   GETTING STARTED   MAKING SOME PROGRESS   MAKING GOOD PROGRESS   DOING IT MOST OF THE TIME   INTEGRATED INTO MY DAILY LIFE

Live the Life
YOU
HAVE IMAGINED!

CHAPTER ELEVEN

MIX UP YOUR DAY

"Variety is the spice of life!" - William Cowper

1. What is your peak performance time? How do you plan it in to your work day?

2. What big project or overwhelming task do you current have that you could "chunk" down to smaller pieces?

3. Have you ever reached the level of non-performance on a task? If so, what did you learn? Do you have ideas on what might work for you to avoid such a situation in the future?

4. What tasks could you put on your "easy tasks" lists to serve as a break from focused work?

5. Would "Focus" days and "Out of the Office" days work for you? What types of tasks would you do on each day?

My Plan to Mix Up the Day:

MIX UP YOUR DAY

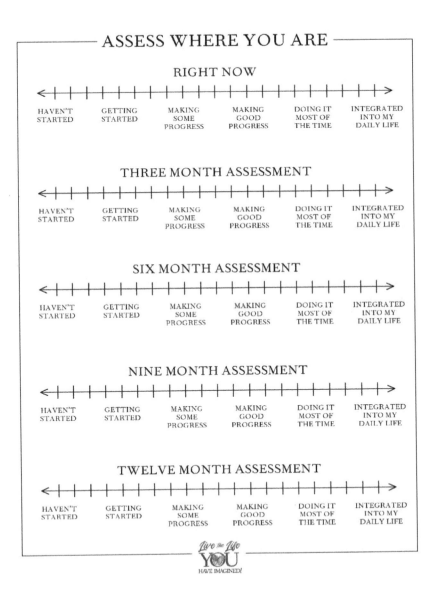

ASSESS WHERE YOU ARE

RIGHT NOW

HAVEN'T STARTED   GETTING STARTED   MAKING SOME PROGRESS   MAKING GOOD PROGRESS   DOING IT MOST OF THE TIME   INTEGRATED INTO MY DAILY LIFE

THREE MONTH ASSESSMENT

HAVEN'T STARTED   GETTING STARTED   MAKING SOME PROGRESS   MAKING GOOD PROGRESS   DOING IT MOST OF THE TIME   INTEGRATED INTO MY DAILY LIFE

SIX MONTH ASSESSMENT

HAVEN'T STARTED   GETTING STARTED   MAKING SOME PROGRESS   MAKING GOOD PROGRESS   DOING IT MOST OF THE TIME   INTEGRATED INTO MY DAILY LIFE

NINE MONTH ASSESSMENT

HAVEN'T STARTED   GETTING STARTED   MAKING SOME PROGRESS   MAKING GOOD PROGRESS   DOING IT MOST OF THE TIME   INTEGRATED INTO MY DAILY LIFE

TWELVE MONTH ASSESSMENT

HAVEN'T STARTED   GETTING STARTED   MAKING SOME PROGRESS   MAKING GOOD PROGRESS   DOING IT MOST OF THE TIME   INTEGRATED INTO MY DAILY LIFE

Live the Life
YOU
HAVE IMAGINED!

63

CHAPTER TWELVE

ELIMINATE CLUTTER

"A place for everything and everything in its place."
- Mrs. Beedon

1. Is your work space organized to be efficient and clutter-free? If not, what could you do to improve it?

2. When you have tried multi-tasking in the past, how did it go? What was the level or accuracy of your work?

3. When you tried focusing on one task at a time, at your own pace, how did that go?

My Plan to Eliminate Clutter:

ELIMINATE CLUTTER

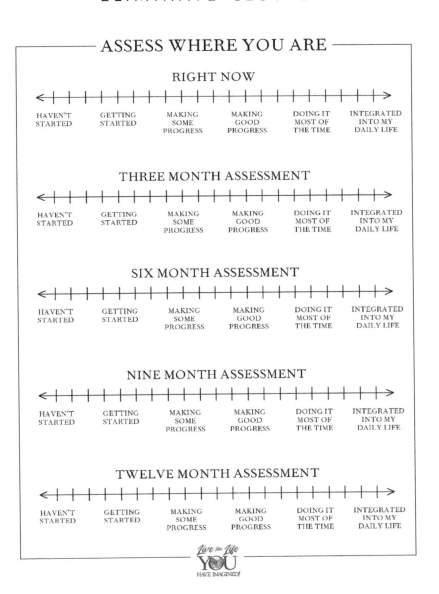

ASSESS WHERE YOU ARE

RIGHT NOW

HAVEN'T STARTED   GETTING STARTED   MAKING SOME PROGRESS   MAKING GOOD PROGRESS   DOING IT MOST OF THE TIME   INTEGRATED INTO MY DAILY LIFE

THREE MONTH ASSESSMENT

HAVEN'T STARTED   GETTING STARTED   MAKING SOME PROGRESS   MAKING GOOD PROGRESS   DOING IT MOST OF THE TIME   INTEGRATED INTO MY DAILY LIFE

SIX MONTH ASSESSMENT

HAVEN'T STARTED   GETTING STARTED   MAKING SOME PROGRESS   MAKING GOOD PROGRESS   DOING IT MOST OF THE TIME   INTEGRATED INTO MY DAILY LIFE

NINE MONTH ASSESSMENT

HAVEN'T STARTED   GETTING STARTED   MAKING SOME PROGRESS   MAKING GOOD PROGRESS   DOING IT MOST OF THE TIME   INTEGRATED INTO MY DAILY LIFE

TWELVE MONTH ASSESSMENT

HAVEN'T STARTED   GETTING STARTED   MAKING SOME PROGRESS   MAKING GOOD PROGRESS   DOING IT MOST OF THE TIME   INTEGRATED INTO MY DAILY LIFE

Live the Life YOU HAVE IMAGINED!

JANIE JURKOVICH

CHAPTER THIRTEEN

BE "IN THE MOMENT"

"Treat every moment as a gift, that is why it is called the present." - Deepak Chopra

1. Have you been guilty of not being "in the moment"? Was it really necessary? If you are guilty of this behavior, what could you do to start to curtail it a bit?

2. Have you experienced being around someone who is constantly using their phone or other technology? How did it make you feel?

3. What sorts of emergencies would you find valid for someone not paying attention at a meeting or event?

4. Have you considered that just because everyone else is checking their phone, that it still might not be courteous to the speaker?

5. Have you considered what you are missing, when you are not present?

My Plan to "Be in The Moment:"

BE "IN THE MOMENT"

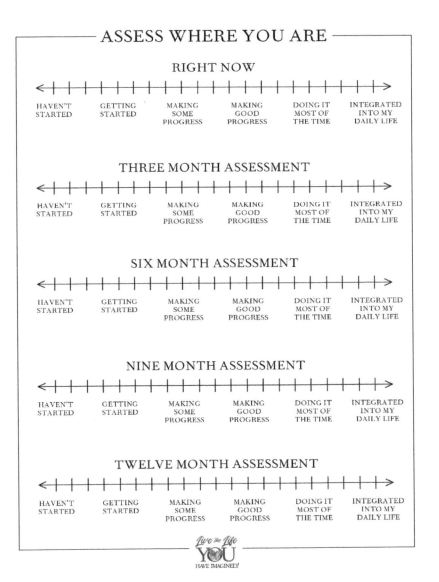

ASSESS WHERE YOU ARE

RIGHT NOW

HAVEN'T STARTED · GETTING STARTED · MAKING SOME PROGRESS · MAKING GOOD PROGRESS · DOING IT MOST OF THE TIME · INTEGRATED INTO MY DAILY LIFE

THREE MONTH ASSESSMENT

HAVEN'T STARTED · GETTING STARTED · MAKING SOME PROGRESS · MAKING GOOD PROGRESS · DOING IT MOST OF THE TIME · INTEGRATED INTO MY DAILY LIFE

SIX MONTH ASSESSMENT

HAVEN'T STARTED · GETTING STARTED · MAKING SOME PROGRESS · MAKING GOOD PROGRESS · DOING IT MOST OF THE TIME · INTEGRATED INTO MY DAILY LIFE

NINE MONTH ASSESSMENT

HAVEN'T STARTED · GETTING STARTED · MAKING SOME PROGRESS · MAKING GOOD PROGRESS · DOING IT MOST OF THE TIME · INTEGRATED INTO MY DAILY LIFE

TWELVE MONTH ASSESSMENT

HAVEN'T STARTED · GETTING STARTED · MAKING SOME PROGRESS · MAKING GOOD PROGRESS · DOING IT MOST OF THE TIME · INTEGRATED INTO MY DAILY LIFE

Live the Life
YOU
HAVE IMAGINED!

71

JANIE JURKOVICH

CHAPTER FOURTEEN

DELEGATE

"For everything we don't like to do, there's someone out there who's really good, wants to do it and will enjoy it." - Josh Kaufman

1. What one task could you delegate right now that would be easy to incorporate into your daily life? How would you go about making this change?
2. If money was no object which tasks would you hire someone to do? Is there a way you could make it happen?
3. Think about the many things you do each day. Are you setting unrealistic standards on any of them? Could you lighten up a bit on some of them? Maybe they don't need to be delegated - just delayed or deleted.

My Plan to Delegate:

DELEGATE

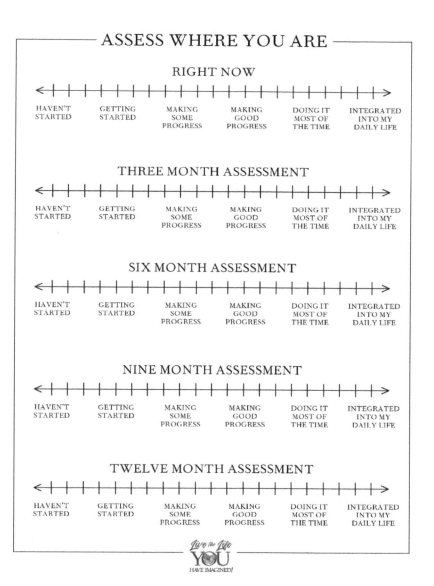

ASSESS WHERE YOU ARE

RIGHT NOW

HAVEN'T STARTED GETTING STARTED MAKING SOME PROGRESS MAKING GOOD PROGRESS DOING IT MOST OF THE TIME INTEGRATED INTO MY DAILY LIFE

THREE MONTH ASSESSMENT

HAVEN'T STARTED GETTING STARTED MAKING SOME PROGRESS MAKING GOOD PROGRESS DOING IT MOST OF THE TIME INTEGRATED INTO MY DAILY LIFE

SIX MONTH ASSESSMENT

HAVEN'T STARTED GETTING STARTED MAKING SOME PROGRESS MAKING GOOD PROGRESS DOING IT MOST OF THE TIME INTEGRATED INTO MY DAILY LIFE

NINE MONTH ASSESSMENT

HAVEN'T STARTED GETTING STARTED MAKING SOME PROGRESS MAKING GOOD PROGRESS DOING IT MOST OF THE TIME INTEGRATED INTO MY DAILY LIFE

TWELVE MONTH ASSESSMENT

HAVEN'T STARTED GETTING STARTED MAKING SOME PROGRESS MAKING GOOD PROGRESS DOING IT MOST OF THE TIME INTEGRATED INTO MY DAILY LIFE

Live the Life YOU HAVE IMAGINED!

JANIE JURKOVICH

CHAPTER FIFTEEN

CHAPTER FIFTEEN

STRETCH YOUR COMFORT ZONE

"Life begins at the end of your comfort zone."
- Neale Donald Walsch

1. Think of a time when you were forced to stretch your comfort zone. How did you feel at first when presented with this challenge? How did you feel once you had met the challenge?
2. Recall a challenge or goal you set for yourself that you met. How did you feel once you accomplished it?
3. Meeting challenges tends to increase our confidence. Do you regularly set your sights on something further once a challenge has been met? If not, what is holding you back?

My Plan to Stretch My Comfort Zone:

STRETCH YOUR COMFORT ZONE

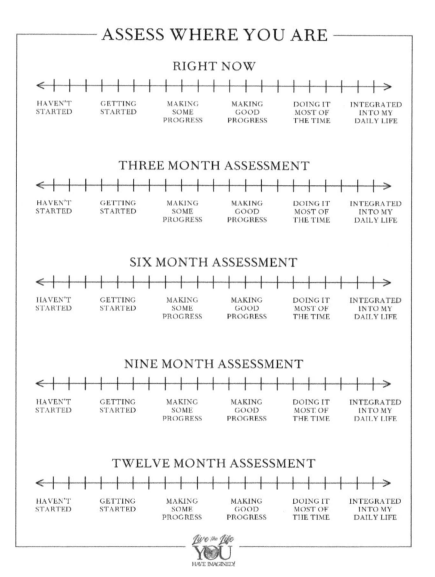

ASSESS WHERE YOU ARE

RIGHT NOW

| HAVEN'T STARTED | GETTING STARTED | MAKING SOME PROGRESS | MAKING GOOD PROGRESS | DOING IT MOST OF THE TIME | INTEGRATED INTO MY DAILY LIFE |

THREE MONTH ASSESSMENT

| HAVEN'T STARTED | GETTING STARTED | MAKING SOME PROGRESS | MAKING GOOD PROGRESS | DOING IT MOST OF THE TIME | INTEGRATED INTO MY DAILY LIFE |

SIX MONTH ASSESSMENT

| HAVEN'T STARTED | GETTING STARTED | MAKING SOME PROGRESS | MAKING GOOD PROGRESS | DOING IT MOST OF THE TIME | INTEGRATED INTO MY DAILY LIFE |

NINE MONTH ASSESSMENT

| HAVEN'T STARTED | GETTING STARTED | MAKING SOME PROGRESS | MAKING GOOD PROGRESS | DOING IT MOST OF THE TIME | INTEGRATED INTO MY DAILY LIFE |

TWELVE MONTH ASSESSMENT

| HAVEN'T STARTED | GETTING STARTED | MAKING SOME PROGRESS | MAKING GOOD PROGRESS | DOING IT MOST OF THE TIME | INTEGRATED INTO MY DAILY LIFE |

Live the Life
YOU
HAVE IMAGINED!

CHAPTER SIXTEEN

PERSEVERANCE

"It's not that I'm so smart, it's just that I stay with problems longer." - Albert Einstein

1. Think about a time when you DID NOT persevere. What happened and how did you feel?

2. Now think about an event when you struggled, kept going and finally persevered. What did you have to go through? What did you accomplish and how did you feel once you got there?

3. When you compare the incidents when you persevered and when you did not - how does that frame how you think about future challenges?

My Plan to Persevere: *(Think about specific situations or goals that could be a challenge for you.)*

PERSEVERANCE

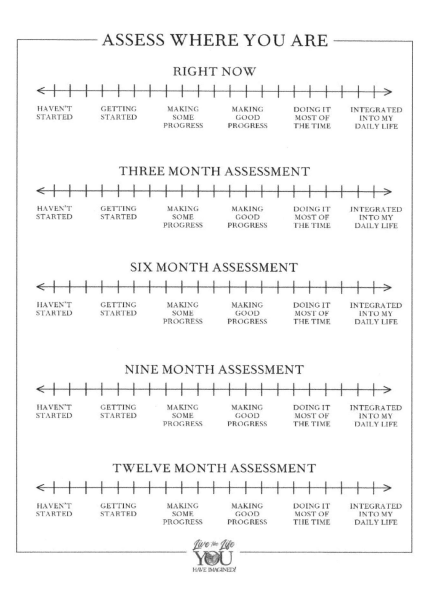

ASSESS WHERE YOU ARE

RIGHT NOW

| HAVEN'T STARTED | GETTING STARTED | MAKING SOME PROGRESS | MAKING GOOD PROGRESS | DOING IT MOST OF THE TIME | INTEGRATED INTO MY DAILY LIFE |

THREE MONTH ASSESSMENT

| HAVEN'T STARTED | GETTING STARTED | MAKING SOME PROGRESS | MAKING GOOD PROGRESS | DOING IT MOST OF THE TIME | INTEGRATED INTO MY DAILY LIFE |

SIX MONTH ASSESSMENT

| HAVEN'T STARTED | GETTING STARTED | MAKING SOME PROGRESS | MAKING GOOD PROGRESS | DOING IT MOST OF THE TIME | INTEGRATED INTO MY DAILY LIFE |

NINE MONTH ASSESSMENT

| HAVEN'T STARTED | GETTING STARTED | MAKING SOME PROGRESS | MAKING GOOD PROGRESS | DOING IT MOST OF THE TIME | INTEGRATED INTO MY DAILY LIFE |

TWELVE MONTH ASSESSMENT

| HAVEN'T STARTED | GETTING STARTED | MAKING SOME PROGRESS | MAKING GOOD PROGRESS | DOING IT MOST OF THE TIME | INTEGRATED INTO MY DAILY LIFE |

Live the Life
YOU
HAVE IMAGINED!

CHAPTER SEVENTEEN

LISTEN TO MUSIC!

"Music produces a kind of pleasure which human nature cannot do without." — Confucius

1. How do you use music in your typical day? What types of music do you listen to?

2. When could you ADD music to your life? What type would you choose?

3. What methods of music do you use? How could you CHANGE your method to better reflect your taste and the type of mood you want to create?

My Plan to Infuse Music into My Life:

LISTEN TO MUSIC!

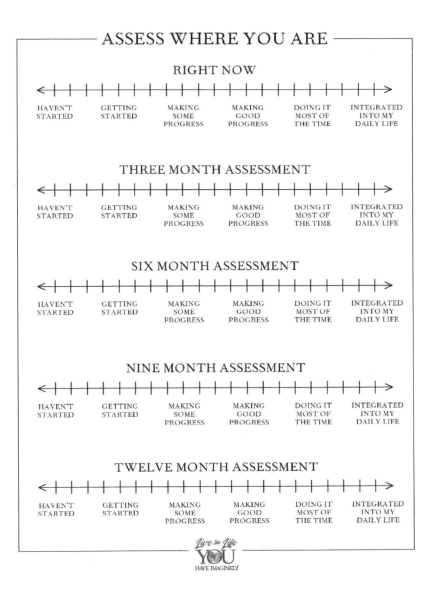

ASSESS WHERE YOU ARE

RIGHT NOW

HAVEN'T STARTED · GETTING STARTED · MAKING SOME PROGRESS · MAKING GOOD PROGRESS · DOING IT MOST OF THE TIME · INTEGRATED INTO MY DAILY LIFE

THREE MONTH ASSESSMENT

HAVEN'T STARTED · GETTING STARTED · MAKING SOME PROGRESS · MAKING GOOD PROGRESS · DOING IT MOST OF THE TIME · INTEGRATED INTO MY DAILY LIFE

SIX MONTH ASSESSMENT

HAVEN'T STARTED · GETTING STARTED · MAKING SOME PROGRESS · MAKING GOOD PROGRESS · DOING IT MOST OF THE TIME · INTEGRATED INTO MY DAILY LIFE

NINE MONTH ASSESSMENT

HAVEN'T STARTED · GETTING STARTED · MAKING SOME PROGRESS · MAKING GOOD PROGRESS · DOING IT MOST OF THE TIME · INTEGRATED INTO MY DAILY LIFE

TWELVE MONTH ASSESSMENT

HAVEN'T STARTED · GETTING STARTED · MAKING SOME PROGRESS · MAKING GOOD PROGRESS · DOING IT MOST OF THE TIME · INTEGRATED INTO MY DAILY LIFE

Live the Life YOU HAVE IMAGINED!

JANIE JURKOVICH

CHAPTER EIGHTEEN

EMBRACE CHANGE!

"When you embrace change you will begin to see it as an opportunity for growth." - Jack Canfield

1. Give some examples of changes you've experienced in your life the last few years.
2. How did you handle one of those "changes?" How could you have handled it differently?
3. Have there been situations where you were more pro-active (or could have been) when dealing with changes?

My Plan for Dealing with Change:

EMBRACE CHANGE!

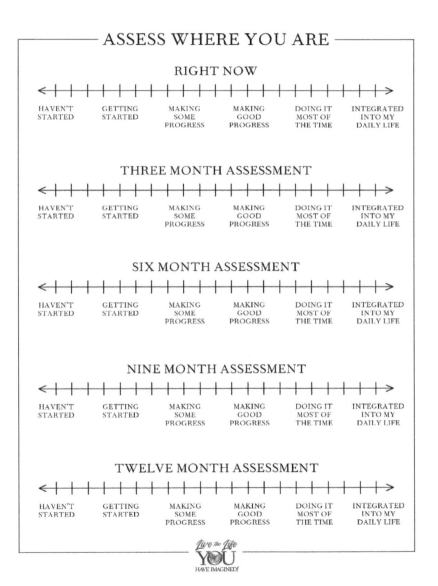

ASSESS WHERE YOU ARE

RIGHT NOW

| HAVEN'T STARTED | GETTING STARTED | MAKING SOME PROGRESS | MAKING GOOD PROGRESS | DOING IT MOST OF THE TIME | INTEGRATED INTO MY DAILY LIFE |

THREE MONTH ASSESSMENT

| HAVEN'T STARTED | GETTING STARTED | MAKING SOME PROGRESS | MAKING GOOD PROGRESS | DOING IT MOST OF THE TIME | INTEGRATED INTO MY DAILY LIFE |

SIX MONTH ASSESSMENT

| HAVEN'T STARTED | GETTING STARTED | MAKING SOME PROGRESS | MAKING GOOD PROGRESS | DOING IT MOST OF THE TIME | INTEGRATED INTO MY DAILY LIFE |

NINE MONTH ASSESSMENT

| HAVEN'T STARTED | GETTING STARTED | MAKING SOME PROGRESS | MAKING GOOD PROGRESS | DOING IT MOST OF THE TIME | INTEGRATED INTO MY DAILY LIFE |

TWELVE MONTH ASSESSMENT

| HAVEN'T STARTED | GETTING STARTED | MAKING SOME PROGRESS | MAKING GOOD PROGRESS | DOING IT MOST OF THE TIME | INTEGRATED INTO MY DAILY LIFE |

Live the Life
YOU
HAVE IMAGINED!

JANIE JURKOVICH

CHAPTER NINETEEN

IGNORE THE NAYSAYERS

"You cannot hang out with negative people and expect to live a positive life." - Joel Olsteen

1. Name a time when you wanted to try something new and were met with negative comments from a friend or relative who just wanted to help you. How did it make you feel. Did their remarks quell your desires?

2. Think about this - do you want the naysayers to direct your life? Do you feel their comments are are necessarily helpful to you?

3. If your naysayer is typically a person in your inner circle, how will you deal with him or her in the future?

My Plan to Deal with Naysayers: *(Use specific examples of comments you expect and how you will handle them.)*

IGNORE THE NAYSAYERS

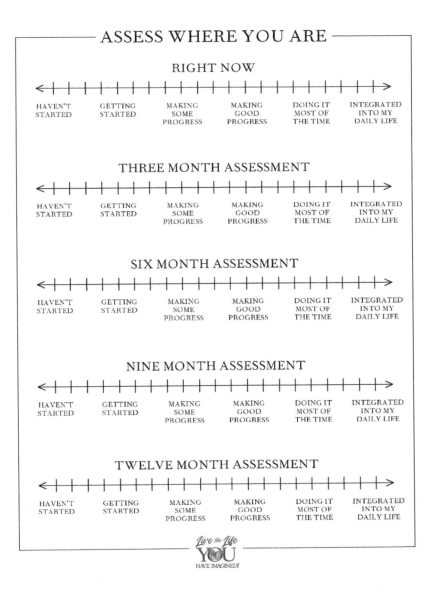

ASSESS WHERE YOU ARE

RIGHT NOW

HAVEN'T STARTED | GETTING STARTED | MAKING SOME PROGRESS | MAKING GOOD PROGRESS | DOING IT MOST OF THE TIME | INTEGRATED INTO MY DAILY LIFE

THREE MONTH ASSESSMENT

HAVEN'T STARTED | GETTING STARTED | MAKING SOME PROGRESS | MAKING GOOD PROGRESS | DOING IT MOST OF THE TIME | INTEGRATED INTO MY DAILY LIFE

SIX MONTH ASSESSMENT

HAVEN'T STARTED | GETTING STARTED | MAKING SOME PROGRESS | MAKING GOOD PROGRESS | DOING IT MOST OF THE TIME | INTEGRATED INTO MY DAILY LIFE

NINE MONTH ASSESSMENT

HAVEN'T STARTED | GETTING STARTED | MAKING SOME PROGRESS | MAKING GOOD PROGRESS | DOING IT MOST OF THE TIME | INTEGRATED INTO MY DAILY LIFE

TWELVE MONTH ASSESSMENT

HAVEN'T STARTED | GETTING STARTED | MAKING SOME PROGRESS | MAKING GOOD PROGRESS | DOING IT MOST OF THE TIME | INTEGRATED INTO MY DAILY LIFE

Live the Life YOU HAVE IMAGINED!

CHAPTER TWENTY

TAKE THE HIGH ROAD

"Take the high road; it's far less crowded."

- Warren Buffett

1. When was the last time you had a conflict with someone? How important was that conflict a week later? A month? A year?

2. Think about a time when you had a serious conflict and the situation escalated due to your actions or the other person's. How did you feel about the situation later?

3. How could the situation have been handled better?

My Plan to Deal with Conflict and Take the High Road:
(Make a list of possible scenarios and write them out as "If 'x' happens, I will do 'y.'")

TAKE THE HIGH ROAD

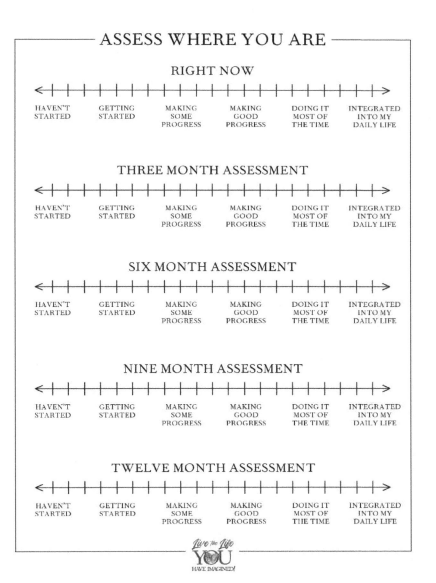

ASSESS WHERE YOU ARE

RIGHT NOW

| HAVEN'T STARTED | GETTING STARTED | MAKING SOME PROGRESS | MAKING GOOD PROGRESS | DOING IT MOST OF THE TIME | INTEGRATED INTO MY DAILY LIFE |

THREE MONTH ASSESSMENT

| HAVEN'T STARTED | GETTING STARTED | MAKING SOME PROGRESS | MAKING GOOD PROGRESS | DOING IT MOST OF THE TIME | INTEGRATED INTO MY DAILY LIFE |

SIX MONTH ASSESSMENT

| HAVEN'T STARTED | GETTING STARTED | MAKING SOME PROGRESS | MAKING GOOD PROGRESS | DOING IT MOST OF THE TIME | INTEGRATED INTO MY DAILY LIFE |

NINE MONTH ASSESSMENT

| HAVEN'T STARTED | GETTING STARTED | MAKING SOME PROGRESS | MAKING GOOD PROGRESS | DOING IT MOST OF THE TIME | INTEGRATED INTO MY DAILY LIFE |

TWELVE MONTH ASSESSMENT

| HAVEN'T STARTED | GETTING STARTED | MAKING SOME PROGRESS | MAKING GOOD PROGRESS | DOING IT MOST OF THE TIME | INTEGRATED INTO MY DAILY LIFE |

Live the Life
YOU
HAVE IMAGINED!

JANIE JURKOVICH

CHAPTER TWENTY-ONE

CHANGE YOUR ATTITUDE

"If you don't like something, change it. If you can't change it, change your attitude." - Maya Angelou

1. Evaluate whether or not you have a positive attitude. What would your close friends say about your attitude?
2. In what areas in your life could your attitude be improved?
3. What method would help you to improve your attitude?

My Plan to Improve My Attitude or Maintain a Positive Attitude:

CHANGE YOUR ATTITUDE

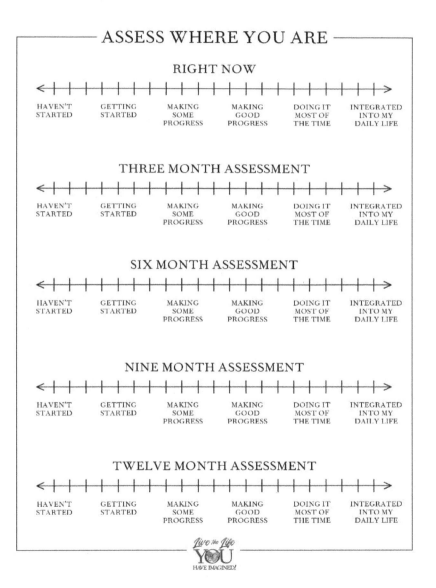

ASSESS WHERE YOU ARE

RIGHT NOW

HAVEN'T STARTED · GETTING STARTED · MAKING SOME PROGRESS · MAKING GOOD PROGRESS · DOING IT MOST OF THE TIME · INTEGRATED INTO MY DAILY LIFE

THREE MONTH ASSESSMENT

HAVEN'T STARTED · GETTING STARTED · MAKING SOME PROGRESS · MAKING GOOD PROGRESS · DOING IT MOST OF THE TIME · INTEGRATED INTO MY DAILY LIFE

SIX MONTH ASSESSMENT

HAVEN'T STARTED · GETTING STARTED · MAKING SOME PROGRESS · MAKING GOOD PROGRESS · DOING IT MOST OF THE TIME · INTEGRATED INTO MY DAILY LIFE

NINE MONTH ASSESSMENT

HAVEN'T STARTED · GETTING STARTED · MAKING SOME PROGRESS · MAKING GOOD PROGRESS · DOING IT MOST OF THE TIME · INTEGRATED INTO MY DAILY LIFE

TWELVE MONTH ASSESSMENT

HAVEN'T STARTED · GETTING STARTED · MAKING SOME PROGRESS · MAKING GOOD PROGRESS · DOING IT MOST OF THE TIME · INTEGRATED INTO MY DAILY LIFE

Live the Life YOU HAVE IMAGINED!

CHAPTER TWENTY-TWO

GIVE GRATITUDE

"Gratitude is a powerful catalyst for happiness. It's the spark that lights a fire of joy in your soul."

- Amy Collette

1. List 5 things you are grateful for (big or small). Don't overthink this. Just write what comes to mind right away.
2. Did you notice any difference in your mood, attitude or feelings after identifying only 5 reasons to be grateful? Can you sense what a difference this could make in your life?
3. How can you fit in a little time each day to be more grateful? When, where and how long could you do this?

My Gratitude Plan: *(Write out specific ways you will live your life more gratefully.)*

GIVE GRATITUDE

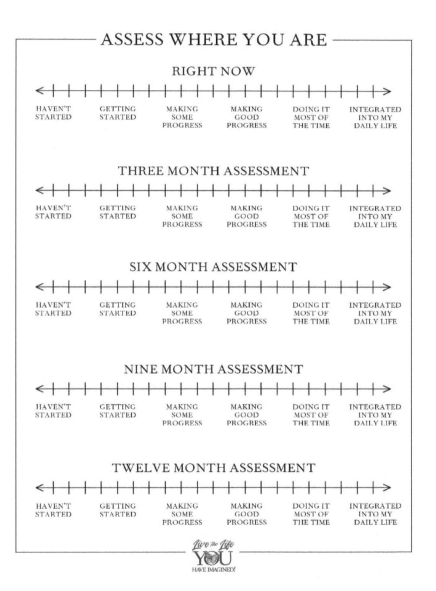

ASSESS WHERE YOU ARE

RIGHT NOW

HAVEN'T STARTED · GETTING STARTED · MAKING SOME PROGRESS · MAKING GOOD PROGRESS · DOING IT MOST OF THE TIME · INTEGRATED INTO MY DAILY LIFE

THREE MONTH ASSESSMENT

HAVEN'T STARTED · GETTING STARTED · MAKING SOME PROGRESS · MAKING GOOD PROGRESS · DOING IT MOST OF THE TIME · INTEGRATED INTO MY DAILY LIFE

SIX MONTH ASSESSMENT

HAVEN'T STARTED · GETTING STARTED · MAKING SOME PROGRESS · MAKING GOOD PROGRESS · DOING IT MOST OF THE TIME · INTEGRATED INTO MY DAILY LIFE

NINE MONTH ASSESSMENT

HAVEN'T STARTED · GETTING STARTED · MAKING SOME PROGRESS · MAKING GOOD PROGRESS · DOING IT MOST OF THE TIME · INTEGRATED INTO MY DAILY LIFE

TWELVE MONTH ASSESSMENT

HAVEN'T STARTED · GETTING STARTED · MAKING SOME PROGRESS · MAKING GOOD PROGRESS · DOING IT MOST OF THE TIME · INTEGRATED INTO MY DAILY LIFE

Live the Life YOU HAVE IMAGINED!

JANIE JURKOVICH

CHAPTER TWENTY-THREE

LOOK FOR THE LESSON

"Experience is a hard teacher because she gives the test first, the lesson afterward." - Vernon Law

1. Think of an unwanted turn your life has taken. When it occurred you were devastated, but how do you feel now?
2. Can you think of any "lessons" you learned from such an experience?

My Plan to Look for the Lesson:

LOOK FOR THE LESSON

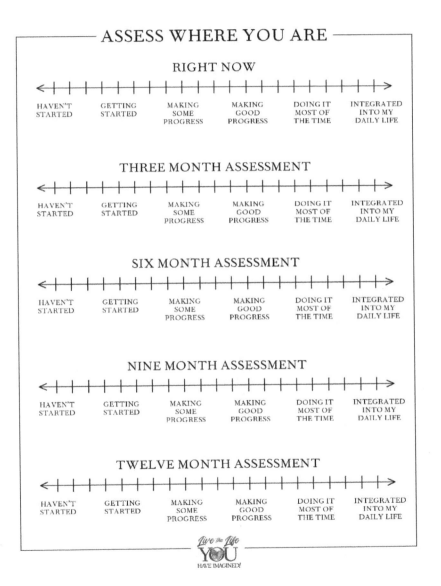

ASSESS WHERE YOU ARE

RIGHT NOW

HAVEN'T STARTED | GETTING STARTED | MAKING SOME PROGRESS | MAKING GOOD PROGRESS | DOING IT MOST OF THE TIME | INTEGRATED INTO MY DAILY LIFE

THREE MONTH ASSESSMENT

HAVEN'T STARTED | GETTING STARTED | MAKING SOME PROGRESS | MAKING GOOD PROGRESS | DOING IT MOST OF THE TIME | INTEGRATED INTO MY DAILY LIFE

SIX MONTH ASSESSMENT

HAVEN'T STARTED | GETTING STARTED | MAKING SOME PROGRESS | MAKING GOOD PROGRESS | DOING IT MOST OF THE TIME | INTEGRATED INTO MY DAILY LIFE

NINE MONTH ASSESSMENT

HAVEN'T STARTED | GETTING STARTED | MAKING SOME PROGRESS | MAKING GOOD PROGRESS | DOING IT MOST OF THE TIME | INTEGRATED INTO MY DAILY LIFE

TWELVE MONTH ASSESSMENT

HAVEN'T STARTED | GETTING STARTED | MAKING SOME PROGRESS | MAKING GOOD PROGRESS | DOING IT MOST OF THE TIME | INTEGRATED INTO MY DAILY LIFE

Live the Life YOU HAVE IMAGINED!

JANIE JURKOVICH

CHAPTER TWENTY-FOUR

RISE TO THE CHALLENGE

"When life throws a curveball, say thank you for the opportunity to learn and grow." - Michelle Maros

1. Name a challenge you met. How did you feel once you accomplished this?
2. Have you ever tried positive self-talk or affirmations? If so, what was the result? If not, are you willing to try it?
3. What is stopping you from setting new challenges and moving forward? What can you do to change that?

My Plan to Meet New Challenges: *(Write specific words and phrases you'll use to encourage youself to meet new challenges.)*

RISE TO THE CHALLENGE

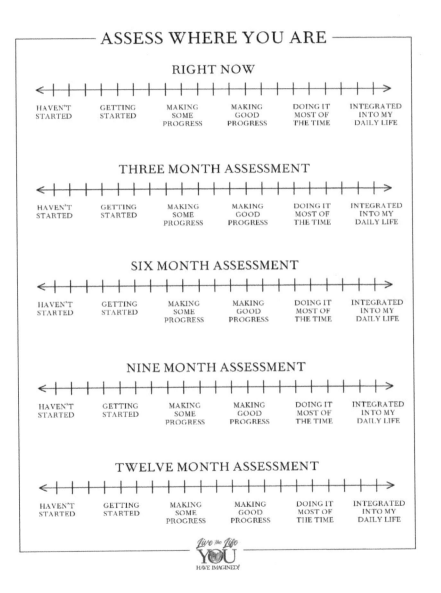

JANIE JURKOVICH

CHAPTER TWENTY-FIVE

LAUGH

"You don't stop laughing because you grow old. You grow old because you stop laughing."
- Michael Pritchard

1. Do you have a "funny friend" who share jakes or comical stories? How do you respond to being around them?

2. Think of a couple quick activities you could do for just 5 minutes a day that would make you laugh. How and when could you incorporate these activities into your life?

3. Do you have a joke in your pocket? One you could tell someone to lift their spirits (or yours)? Look or listen for a good one. Practice it and then share. (If you're desperate to find a good joke, look online or call Zappos. They have a Joke of the Day!)

My Plan to Add Laughter to My Life:

LAUGH

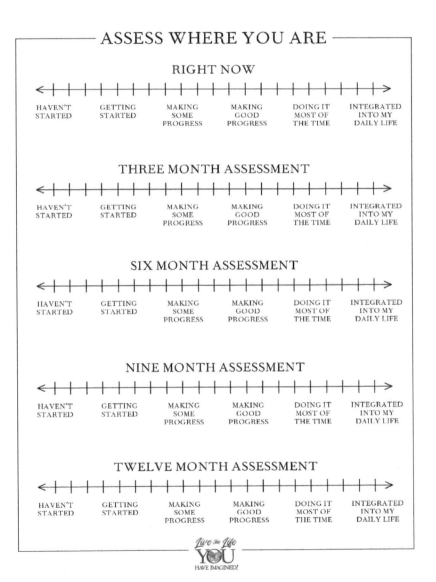

ASSESS WHERE YOU ARE

RIGHT NOW

HAVEN'T STARTED · GETTING STARTED · MAKING SOME PROGRESS · MAKING GOOD PROGRESS · DOING IT MOST OF THE TIME · INTEGRATED INTO MY DAILY LIFE

THREE MONTH ASSESSMENT

HAVEN'T STARTED · GETTING STARTED · MAKING SOME PROGRESS · MAKING GOOD PROGRESS · DOING IT MOST OF THE TIME · INTEGRATED INTO MY DAILY LIFE

SIX MONTH ASSESSMENT

HAVEN'T STARTED · GETTING STARTED · MAKING SOME PROGRESS · MAKING GOOD PROGRESS · DOING IT MOST OF THE TIME · INTEGRATED INTO MY DAILY LIFE

NINE MONTH ASSESSMENT

HAVEN'T STARTED · GETTING STARTED · MAKING SOME PROGRESS · MAKING GOOD PROGRESS · DOING IT MOST OF THE TIME · INTEGRATED INTO MY DAILY LIFE

TWELVE MONTH ASSESSMENT

HAVEN'T STARTED · GETTING STARTED · MAKING SOME PROGRESS · MAKING GOOD PROGRESS · DOING IT MOST OF THE TIME · INTEGRATED INTO MY DAILY LIFE

JANIE JURKOVICH

CHAPTER TWENTY-SIX
WEALTH-GO & GET IT!

"Wealth is the ability to fully experience life."
- Henry David Thoreau

1. Do you have any guilt about monetary wealth? How can you re-frame your self-talk to relieve that guilt?
2. How would additional monies improve your life?
3. If money was no object, what would you do differently in your everyday life? (Dream a little here.)

My Plan to Think of Wealth as a Positive Force in My Life:

WEALTH - GO & GET IT!

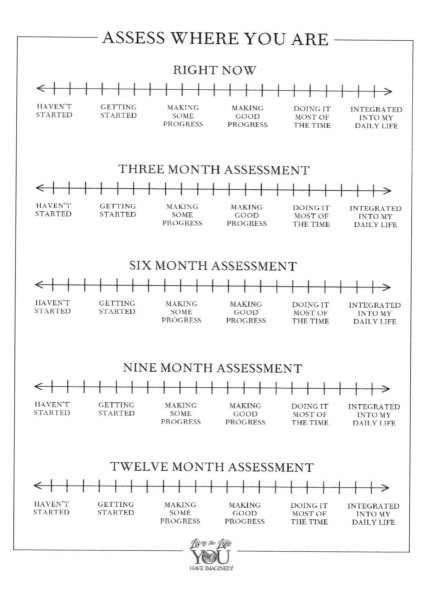

ASSESS WHERE YOU ARE

RIGHT NOW

HAVEN'T STARTED   GETTING STARTED   MAKING SOME PROGRESS   MAKING GOOD PROGRESS   DOING IT MOST OF THE TIME   INTEGRATED INTO MY DAILY LIFE

THREE MONTH ASSESSMENT

HAVEN'T STARTED   GETTING STARTED   MAKING SOME PROGRESS   MAKING GOOD PROGRESS   DOING IT MOST OF THE TIME   INTEGRATED INTO MY DAILY LIFE

SIX MONTH ASSESSMENT

HAVEN'T STARTED   GETTING STARTED   MAKING SOME PROGRESS   MAKING GOOD PROGRESS   DOING IT MOST OF THE TIME   INTEGRATED INTO MY DAILY LIFE

NINE MONTH ASSESSMENT

HAVEN'T STARTED   GETTING STARTED   MAKING SOME PROGRESS   MAKING GOOD PROGRESS   DOING IT MOST OF THE TIME   INTEGRATED INTO MY DAILY LIFE

TWELVE MONTH ASSESSMENT

HAVEN'T STARTED   GETTING STARTED   MAKING SOME PROGRESS   MAKING GOOD PROGRESS   DOING IT MOST OF THE TIME   INTEGRATED INTO MY DAILY LIFE

Live the Life
YOU
HAVE IMAGINED!

123

JANIE JURKOVICH

CHAPTER TWENTY-SEVEN

DELETE TV FROM YOUR LIFE

"I find television very educating. Every time somebody turns on the set, I go into the other room and read a book." - Groucho Marx

1. What are your favorite TV shows? Is there a pattern of junk, news, or channel surfing?
2. How many hours of TV do you typically watch each week? How much time does TV eat up in each day?
3. What activities could you be doing instead of watching TV?

My Plan to Delete or Reduce TV-Watching:

DELETE TV FROM YOUR LIFE

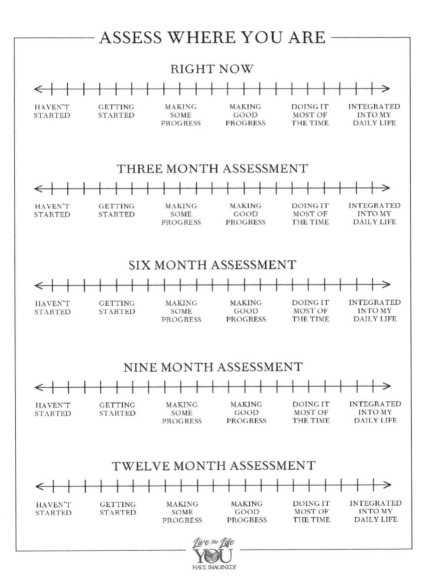

ASSESS WHERE YOU ARE

RIGHT NOW

| HAVEN'T STARTED | GETTING STARTED | MAKING SOME PROGRESS | MAKING GOOD PROGRESS | DOING IT MOST OF THE TIME | INTEGRATED INTO MY DAILY LIFE |

THREE MONTH ASSESSMENT

| HAVEN'T STARTED | GETTING STARTED | MAKING SOME PROGRESS | MAKING GOOD PROGRESS | DOING IT MOST OF THE TIME | INTEGRATED INTO MY DAILY LIFE |

SIX MONTH ASSESSMENT

| HAVEN'T STARTED | GETTING STARTED | MAKING SOME PROGRESS | MAKING GOOD PROGRESS | DOING IT MOST OF THE TIME | INTEGRATED INTO MY DAILY LIFE |

NINE MONTH ASSESSMENT

| HAVEN'T STARTED | GETTING STARTED | MAKING SOME PROGRESS | MAKING GOOD PROGRESS | DOING IT MOST OF THE TIME | INTEGRATED INTO MY DAILY LIFE |

TWELVE MONTH ASSESSMENT

| HAVEN'T STARTED | GETTING STARTED | MAKING SOME PROGRESS | MAKING GOOD PROGRESS | DOING IT MOST OF THE TIME | INTEGRATED INTO MY DAILY LIFE |

Live the Life YOU HAVE IMAGINED!

127

JANIE JURKOVICH

CHAPTER TWENTY-EIGHT

FIND AND FOLLOW YOUR BLISS

"Follow your bliss and the universe will open doors
for you where there were only walls."
- Joseph Campbell

1. What things, people or activities bring you joy?
2. What things, people or activities definitely DO NOT bring you joy, but other people may like?
3. How can you consciously select/edit your activities to reach a more blissful life?

My Plan to Find and Follow my Bliss:

FIND AND FOLLOW YOUR BLISS

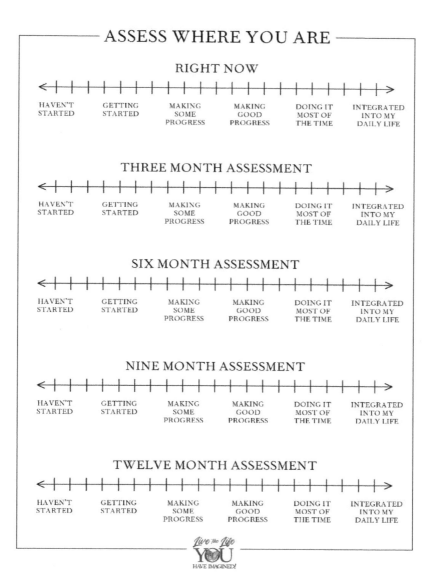

CHAPTER TWENTY-NINE

WORK ON SELF-DEVELOPMENT

"An investment in knowledge pays the best interest."

- Benjamin Franklin

1. What would you like to learn to do better in your work life?

2. What would you like to learn to do better in your personal life?

3. How could you find out more about the above two topics? Make a list of possible actions you could take right away.

My Self-Development Plan:

WORK ON SELF-DEVELOPMENT

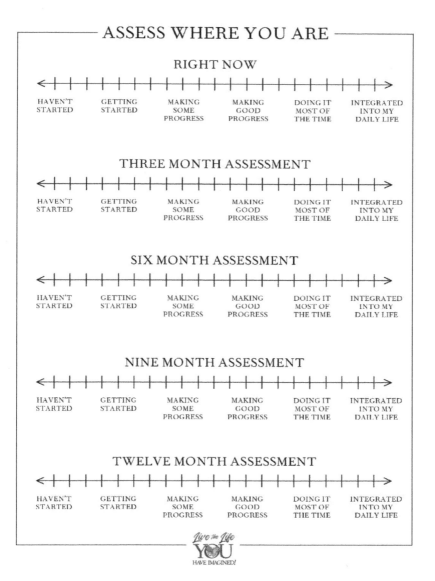

ASSESS WHERE YOU ARE

RIGHT NOW

HAVEN'T STARTED — GETTING STARTED — MAKING SOME PROGRESS — MAKING GOOD PROGRESS — DOING IT MOST OF THE TIME — INTEGRATED INTO MY DAILY LIFE

THREE MONTH ASSESSMENT

HAVEN'T STARTED — GETTING STARTED — MAKING SOME PROGRESS — MAKING GOOD PROGRESS — DOING IT MOST OF THE TIME — INTEGRATED INTO MY DAILY LIFE

SIX MONTH ASSESSMENT

HAVEN'T STARTED — GETTING STARTED — MAKING SOME PROGRESS — MAKING GOOD PROGRESS — DOING IT MOST OF THE TIME — INTEGRATED INTO MY DAILY LIFE

NINE MONTH ASSESSMENT

HAVEN'T STARTED — GETTING STARTED — MAKING SOME PROGRESS — MAKING GOOD PROGRESS — DOING IT MOST OF THE TIME — INTEGRATED INTO MY DAILY LIFE

TWELVE MONTH ASSESSMENT

HAVEN'T STARTED — GETTING STARTED — MAKING SOME PROGRESS — MAKING GOOD PROGRESS — DOING IT MOST OF THE TIME — INTEGRATED INTO MY DAILY LIFE

Live the Life
YOU
HAVE IMAGINED!

135

JANIE JURKOVICH

CHAPTER THIRTY

REALIZE LIFE IS A JOURNEY

"Life is a journey, not a destination."
- *Ralph Waldo Emerson*

1. What affirmation or self-talk can you write down now to refer to later, in time of stress and doubt, when you might consider giving up?
2. Write a list of reasons WHY it's important to you to live your best life, one where you are truly happy and fulfilled.

My Plan to Keep on Course Through the Journey of Life:

REALIZE LIFE IS A JOURNEY

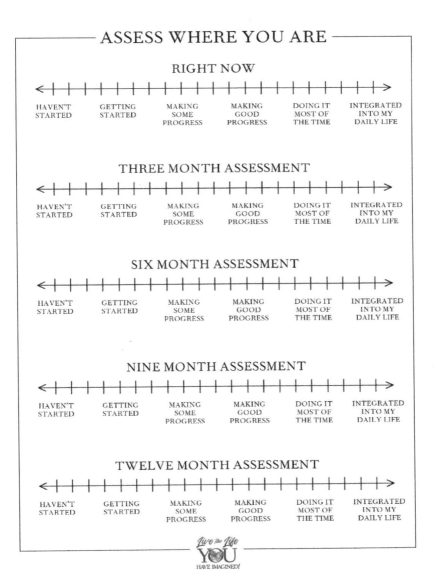

ASSESS WHERE YOU ARE

RIGHT NOW

HAVEN'T STARTED · GETTING STARTED · MAKING SOME PROGRESS · MAKING GOOD PROGRESS · DOING IT MOST OF THE TIME · INTEGRATED INTO MY DAILY LIFE

THREE MONTH ASSESSMENT

HAVEN'T STARTED · GETTING STARTED · MAKING SOME PROGRESS · MAKING GOOD PROGRESS · DOING IT MOST OF THE TIME · INTEGRATED INTO MY DAILY LIFE

SIX MONTH ASSESSMENT

HAVEN'T STARTED · GETTING STARTED · MAKING SOME PROGRESS · MAKING GOOD PROGRESS · DOING IT MOST OF THE TIME · INTEGRATED INTO MY DAILY LIFE

NINE MONTH ASSESSMENT

HAVEN'T STARTED · GETTING STARTED · MAKING SOME PROGRESS · MAKING GOOD PROGRESS · DOING IT MOST OF THE TIME · INTEGRATED INTO MY DAILY LIFE

TWELVE MONTH ASSESSMENT

HAVEN'T STARTED · GETTING STARTED · MAKING SOME PROGRESS · MAKING GOOD PROGRESS · DOING IT MOST OF THE TIME · INTEGRATED INTO MY DAILY LIFE

Live the Life YOU HAVE IMAGINED!

JANIE JURKOVICH

CHAPTER THIRTY-ONE

THE NECESSARY COMPONENTS

"The good life is a process, not a state of being. It is a direction not a destination." - Carl Rogers

1. What have you learned by going through this process? Any newfound direction for your life? Are you ready to go off of "auto-pilot"?

2. Are you willing to do what it takes to make these changes? What is your motivation?

My Plan to Keep on Course Through the Journey of Life:

THE NECESSARY COMPONENTS

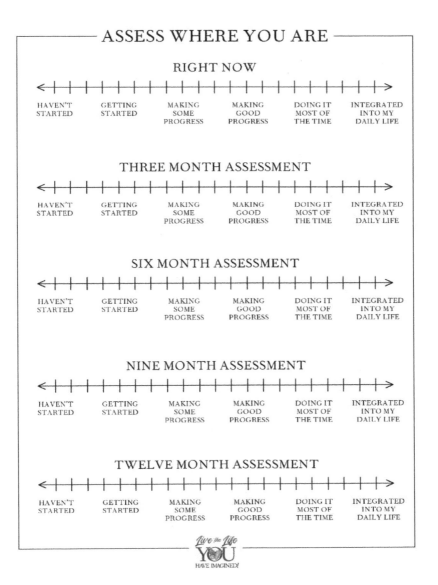

ASSESS WHERE YOU ARE

RIGHT NOW

HAVEN'T STARTED   GETTING STARTED   MAKING SOME PROGRESS   MAKING GOOD PROGRESS   DOING IT MOST OF THE TIME   INTEGRATED INTO MY DAILY LIFE

THREE MONTH ASSESSMENT

HAVEN'T STARTED   GETTING STARTED   MAKING SOME PROGRESS   MAKING GOOD PROGRESS   DOING IT MOST OF THE TIME   INTEGRATED INTO MY DAILY LIFE

SIX MONTH ASSESSMENT

HAVEN'T STARTED   GETTING STARTED   MAKING SOME PROGRESS   MAKING GOOD PROGRESS   DOING IT MOST OF THE TIME   INTEGRATED INTO MY DAILY LIFE

NINE MONTH ASSESSMENT

HAVEN'T STARTED   GETTING STARTED   MAKING SOME PROGRESS   MAKING GOOD PROGRESS   DOING IT MOST OF THE TIME   INTEGRATED INTO MY DAILY LIFE

TWELVE MONTH ASSESSMENT

HAVEN'T STARTED   GETTING STARTED   MAKING SOME PROGRESS   MAKING GOOD PROGRESS   DOING IT MOST OF THE TIME   INTEGRATED INTO MY DAILY LIFE

Live the Life YOU HAVE IMAGINED!

JANIE JURKOVICH

MORE MOTIVATION

"When You Think of Quitting,
Remember Why You Started"
- John Di Lemme

I have this printed on a 4x6 card and I've placed it in visible spots whenever more motivation is necessary. I've left you enough room that you can snap a photo with your phone. Make it your wallpaper or screensaver for a regular reminder.

JANIE JURKOVICH

AFTERWORD

I never imagined that after 35 years of marriage and devoting my life to the care of my children, my home, my spouse and my job, that I would find myself divorced, lost and wondering what happened.

Then, I never imagined that four years later I would have been a published author (twice!), traveled to Egypt, Portugal and France, and won medals in regional masters-level track and field competitions.

This time I don't have to wonder what happened. I have intently read, reflected and explored. Then I set out to deliberately and intentionally build this life.

And I'm not done yet. I'm still exploring, growing and going further down the path in this journey.

I'm so glad you've come along with me! No matter where you

started, you're now further along and are closer than ever before to living the life you always imagined.

Maybe you're living that life and now you're thinking even bigger and better. Keep dreaming and keep working hard. You can do this!

I want to hear from you about your successes and your setbacks. Reach out to me at **JanieJ@JanieJ.net**

Here's to you and the life you have imagined.

Janie J

WHAT TO DO NEXT

Congratulations on working your way all the way through the "Live the Life You Have Imagined Companion Journal."

Don't put this back on the shelf! Keep it near you to remind yourself of how hard you're working to start living the life you've always imagined. And if you haven't already, go put a reminder on your calendar for three, six and twelve months from now to review your progress.

Do you belong to an organization or association that would like to hear my story and have me inspire and motivate your team or members in person? Contact me at **JanieJ@JanieJ.net**

JANIE JURKOVICH

GET YOUR FREE BONUS

Remember, if you want to have more room to write, I've put all of the "Discussion Questions" together in one, easy-to-print downloadable document which you can use to write down and review your answers and plans.

Go to **www.JanieJ.net/bonus** to get yours now.
Go to **www.JanieJ.net/bonus2** to get the My Habits and My Successes blank sheets.

Plus, you'll receive a free excerpt of my forthcoming book "Single and Sixty," a reflective and sometimes humorous journey of one woman's quest to deal with divorce later in life.

JANIE JURKOVICH

CONTRIBUTORS

Marketing consulting and editing by Beth Bridges,
TheNetworkingMotivator.com

Logo, cover design and charts by Ellie Dote,
EllieGirlCreations.com

Interior design by Bryan Keith Pfeifer

Author photo by Suzanne Moles, **WattleWeb.com**